Enchanting
MYANMAR

MICK SHIPPEN

JOHN BEAUFOY PUBLISHING

Contents

Above: Buddhist monks waiting for a donation of food at Ganayon Kyaung Temple, Amarapura near Mandalay.

Above left: A fisherman on Inle Lake checking his nets in the early evening. The lake is one of the country's most popular travel destinations.

Above right: Nuts and 'lahpet', pickled tea, for sale in Hledan Market, Yangon. The tea is eaten as a snack.

Opposite: The ancient zedis of Bagan are one of Myanmar's many wonders.

Title page: The Golden Rock, also known as Mount Kyaikhtiyo, is one of Myanmar's most sacred Buddhist sites and a mesmerizing sight when illuminated at night.

Chapter 1: The Land of Golden Zedis

In 1898, in "Letters from the East" Rudyard Kipling, recounting his journey by steamer sailing up the Irrawaddy Delta to Rangoon, wrote "Then, a golden mystery upheaved itself on the horizon…a shape that was neither Muslim dome nor Hindu temple spire…the golden dome said: 'This is Burma, and it will be quite unlike any land you know about.'" The celebrated English novelist and poet was describing his first view of the region's most sacred Buddhist site, the Shwedagon Paya, a magnificent 99-m (325-ft) gilded zedi crowning Singuttara Hill.

Right: The rather grand City Hall in central Yangon dates from 1936.

Below: The Shwedagon Paya is a highlight of any visit to Yangon. The pinnacle of the zedi is encrusted with 2,317 rubies and 5448 diamonds.

Today, over a century since Kipling's observations, the country now known as Myanmar is the last frontier of discovery for cultural travellers in South-East Asia. An intriguing land of shimmering temple spires and archaeological wonders, extraordinary ethnic diversity, astonishing natural beauty, and warm and welcoming people, this 'golden land' still remains unlike any other.

The gateway to Myanmar is the former capital, Yangon (known to the British as Rangoon). Here, the faded glory of imposing British architecture draws the admiration of visitors but is also a pertinent reminder of a more enduring colonial-era legacy – a turbulent history. Yet the youthful population now looks forward and on the city's bustling streets there is a palpable sense of optimism. Today's Yangon is a city of contrast. Buildings of red-brick and crumbling stucco are fronted by billboards advertising the latest 'must-have' gadgets while Buddhist mantras of non-attachment are whispered within the confines of sacred temples; muscular SUVs with blacked-out windows roll past ageing trishaws laden with smiling ladies cradling fresh produce from the market; street vendors sell posters of Aung San and his daughter Aung San Suu Kyi while editorials in the state newspaper, *The New Light of Myanmar*, declare the 'people's desires'. Unchanged yet looking to the future, chaotic with pockets of calm, deeply complex yet often starkly black and white, Yangon's heady cocktail is as refreshing as it is intoxicating.

Above: *Many of Yangon's architectural gems from the colonial-era are partially covered with billboards resulting in an intriguing blend of old and new.*

Below: In rural Myanmar, life moves at a slower pace than elsewhere. Bullock carts are still a common means of transport.

Right: At Bagan, hundreds of zedis are scattered across a vast area. As the evening light fades, the brickwork of the crumbling temples takes on a warm glow.

In rural Myanmar time is marked by the slow turn of bullock cart wheels, the seasonal rhythm of "sow and reap" in the paddy fields and by a calendar of religious festivals and boisterous temple fairs. It is here, beyond Yangon, that Myanmar's true beauty and character are revealed. In Bagan and Mrauk U, ancient zedis (Buddhist shrines containing sacred relics) dating from the 11th century stand in testament to Myanmar's past splendours and as inspiration for travellers of our time. The mere mention of Mandalay still has the power to conjure up images of an exotic and unfamiliar land, of sweltering nights beneath a mosquito net and a lazy ceiling fan, and flotillas of paddle steamers drifting down the Ayeyarwaddy River (known to the British as the Irrawaddy). After exploring the burgeoning city's many nearby sights such as U Bein, the world's longest teak bridge, and the zedi-strewn Sagaing Hill, travellers can board a luxurious cruise ship and sail down the mighty river. Further north, leg rowers, jumping temple cats and the floating gardens of Inle Lake provide a glimpse of local curiosities and unique traditions, while further north still hill tribes and pristine forests are a draw for cultural tourists and nature lovers.

Above: *A fisherman on Inle Lake using the unique leg-rowing technique while setting his nets.*

Below: *The 70-m (230-ft) reclining Buddha at Chauk Htat Gyi Temple in Yangon was built in the mid-60s to replace an earthquake-damaged image.*

No visit to the country is complete without making a pilgrimage to the precariously balanced Golden Rock and to the two monumental reclining Buddha images at Bago. While the perfect end to a memorable journey can be found at idyllic resorts in Ngapali, an undeveloped coastline of pristine beaches where fishermen cast their nets wide into azure waters.

The combination of Myanmar's beauty and diversity, its rich culture and history, and its charming people make it one of Asia's most rewarding and truly enchanting destinations. Discovery awaits.

Geography and Climate

Situated on the western edge of South-East Asia, Myanmar encompasses an area of 677,000 km² (261,228 sq. miles), making it the second largest nation in the region after Indonesia. The country spans 936 km (581 miles) from east to west and 2,051 km (1,275 miles) from north to south, sharing its borders with Thailand and Lao PDR to the east, China to the north-east, and India and Bangladesh to the north-west. Myanmar's extensive coastline runs for 2,800 km (1,740 miles) along the Andaman Sea, the Gulf of Mottama (formerly known as the Gulf of Martaban) and the Bay of Bengal.

Below: Rolling hills and the valley surrounding Mandalay seen from the road to the former British hill station of Pyin U Lwin.

Left: The boat from Sittwe to Mrauk U passes through a beautiful and fertile landscape where rural subsistence farmers catch fish, harvest rice and tend buffalo.

Below: Myanmar's forests are home to an incredible diversity of wild orchids.

Myanmar also shares a 2,204-km (1,370-mile) land border with China and an extensive 1,338-km (831-mile) land border with India. It is perfectly situated to act as the gateway to Central Asia and to benefit from the region's rapid development.

Rich in natural resources, Myanmar has huge potential for growth. For many years, China has been the country's largest trade partner and investor, supplying consumer goods, durables, machinery and equipment, while importing Myanmar's timber, agricultural produce and minerals, such as coal, tin, zinc, marble and limestone. However, it is the possibility of large-scale discoveries of oil and gas that could see Myanmar quickly become a major supplier to neighbouring, energy-thirsty nations.

A rural nation comprising 14 states, Myanmar is blessed with a range of landscapes, flora and fauna. Vast tracts of forest are home to incredible biodiversity and wildlife, such as elephants, tigers, leopards, flying squirrels, porcupines, gibbons, black bears and 52 types of poisonous snake. Unique animals include the Red Panda and the Myanmar Snub-nosed Monkey, a species only discovered in 2010. Found in Kachin State in north-eastern Myanmar, the monkey is already under serious threat from increased logging and development. It is thought the population is only around 300 individuals.

Teak forests thrive in the mountainous northern reaches of Myanmar and the country holds 75% of the world's reserves. Wild orchids can also be found in great profusion and there are 841 recorded species. However, populations are said to be dramatically declining as a result of logging and an illegal trade with collectors.

In the far northern Kachin State, at the foot of the Himalayas, mountain peaks rise to almost 6,000 m (20,000 ft) and primary forest still stands. It is from here that the lifeblood of Myanmar, the mighty Ayeyarwaddy, winds its way south for 2,000 km (1,242 miles), fertilizing the country's rice bowl as it does so, eventually spilling out into the delta. Other major rivers include the Chindwin which starts its journey in the northern state of Sagaing flowing down to meet the Ayeyarwaddy between Mandalay and Bagan, and the Thanlwin (also known as the Salween) which makes its way through Shan, Kayah, Kayin and Mon states, for a time serving as a natural border with Thailand, before finally emptying into the Gulf of Mottama. To the west and south of the delta are white sand beaches and pristine tropical islands.

Above: A fleet of small fishing boats in a tributary of Yangon River waiting for high tide.

Below: A farmer near Sittwe in western Myanmar cutting and bunching sheaves of rice during November's harvest.

Myanmar enjoys a monsoon climate with three seasons. The rains last from May to October, the cool season from November to February and the hot season from March to June. Torrential rains can make travel during the monsoon season difficult as many roads are not sealed. The highland regions usually enjoy a longer period of pleasantly cool weather while in the central plains the season of extremely hot, dry weather is extended. The delta and coastal regions are the most humid. The mean annual temperature is 27°C (81°F) with average daily temperatures in Yangon ranging from 18–32°C (64–90°F) in the cool season and from 30–38°C (86–100°F) in April during the hot season.

Below: For years the coastline of Ngapali Beach has remained an idyllic getaway but it seems destined to become a major tourist hotspot lined with resorts.

Right: Two girls, their faces covered in tanaka powder, trawl the marshland around Inle Lake for freshwater shrimps and small fish.

A Brief History of Myanmar

Myanmar's fascinating and often turbulent history charts the glorious golden period of Bagan, raging battles with neighbouring Thailand, Anglo-Burmese wars and years of British colonialism, a struggle for independence, and a period of self-imposed isolationism followed by optimism for a brighter future.

Below: The 12th-century Dhamma Yin Zi Ka Pagoda in Bagan has pentagonal terraces instead of the usual Bagan-style square base.

Early History

Archaeological evidence of human habitation in Myanmar dates back to 2,500 B.C. The first recorded settlers were the Pyu who migrated into northern Myanmar in the second century B.C. and established several city states. By the eighth century the Pyu capital of Halingyi was destroyed by marauding forces from the Nanzhao kingdom in southern China. In around the sixth century, the Mon who are believed to have migrated from east India, established a kingdom known as Suvarnabhumi or the Golden Land around Bago. They are also credited with bringing religion and their distinctive arts to Myanmar, however, many written works were destroyed during violent conflicts with the Bamar.

The First Empires

Some 1,500 years ago, the Bamar, who originated in what is now Yunnan in China, migrated down the Ayeryarwaddy river valley and into Upper Myanmar, eventually replacing the ethnic Mon as the dominant presence in the area. In the ninth century, the Bamar established settlements just north of Mandalay before founding Bagan. The Bagan period is known as the Golden Age of Myanmar history. Following the conversion of King Anawrahta to Buddhism, his army engaged in a sortie against the Mon king, Manuha, taking Buddhist scriptures and relics, and capturing monks. Securing victory over the Mon in 1057, the Bamar entered a period of religious fervour during which many of Bagan's greatest temples were built and it became the capital of the country's first empire. Architectural gems of the period include the Shwezigon Paya and the Shwesandaw Paya.

By the mid 13th century Bagan was already in serious decline and when it eventually fell to invading Mongol troops in 1289, the country was divided into rival states, including Ava (also known as Inwa) which remained the capital until it was sacked by the Shan in 1527.

Top: Towering above the other monuments of Bagan, the magnificent white Thatbyinnyu Temple was built for King Alaungsithu who reigned from 1113 to 1163.

Above: One of the four enormous Buddha images at Kyaik Pun Paya in Bago.

Right: Buddha images and wall paintings inside Nagayon Paya, Bagan.

In 1550, King Bayinnaung unified disparate kingdoms and led a successful attack on Siam, present-day Thailand. However, following the king's death, Myanmar's second kingdom quickly declined. By this time the Mon had established a presence in Ava, only to be displaced by King Alaungpaya in 1752. After a short eight year reign, the king died at just 46 years of age and was succeeded by his son, Hsinbyushin.

Between 1759 and 1824, Myanmar's Konbaung Dynasty grew in strength and confidence. Establishing a new capital in Yangon, it sought to spread its influence in Arakan (present-day Rakhine State) and Assam in India but by doing so drew the wrath of the British Empire.

The British in Myanmar

Determined to expand their territory and secure a bounty of natural resources, the British instigated the Anglo-Burmese war of 1852, taking control of the south. After further conflict in 1885, they wrestled Mandalay from the last royal, King Thibaw and brought the entire country under the control of the Empire.

Britain is said to have found Myanmar the hardest country within the Empire to control. The problem lay with the majority Bamar rather than the other indigenous groups who were granted relative autonomy over their states by the British (a factor which has been attributed to recent conflicts and struggles for independence by the Karen and Shan). While the British helped themselves to teak, oil, gems, rice and other resources, resistance from the Bamar grew.

In 1938, as protests escalated, British police killed a university student during a demonstration and in another incident, British soldiers fired into a monk-led protest in Mandalay, killing 17 people. A number of monks also died in prison. As strife within the country continued, the British Empire separated Myanmar's administration from India but more trouble followed including violence by the Bamar against Indian and Chinese settlers brought in by the British.

One student involved in protests was Bogyoke Aung San, Aung San Suu Kyi's father. As part of a group known as the '30 Comrades', he sought support for the independence movement, eventually receiving training from the Japanese for his Burmese National Army. Aung San aligned himself with invading Japanese forces during WWII as they tried to push the British out of Myanmar. However, after witnessing the brutality of the Japanese, he realized that he had jumped out of the frying pan and into the fire and switched allegiance to the Allied forces. The Chindit Campaign against the Japanese followed at a cost of 27,000 Allied soldiers' lives.

Opposite: *A short distance from Mandalay the crumbling zedis at Inwa are a reminder of the ancient capital's former glories.*

Above: *Many of Yangon's splendid colonial-era buildings are in need of restoration.*

Continuing Strife

In 1947, Aung San signed papers in London to guarantee self-rule. At elections his Anti-Fascist People's Party secured a convincing victory against the Bamar opposition led by U Saw, who took just three seats. Shortly after, Aung San and six of his cabinet were gunned down and in 1948 U Saw was convicted and hanged for the murders by the British.

From 1948 to 1962, there was widespread conflict and internal struggle in Myanmar, and in 1958 Prime Minister U Nu accepted 18 months of military rule to restore order. In 1962 General Ne Win led a military coup, abolished the constitution and established socialist economic policies that were to have disastrous consequences on the economy. Ne Win went on to create the Burma Socialist Program Party (BSPP), the only political party allowed in the country.

In 1974, at the funeral of former UN Secretary General U Thant in Yangon, student demonstrations broke out and, in an act that echoed the British crackdown of 1938, ended in government troops storming a university campus, killing several students and declaring martial law.

During mass demonstrations on August 8, 1988, military forces turned on demonstrators. Following the violence, Aung San Suu Kyi made her first political speech and became leader of the opposition. That year, a group of generals deposed Ne Win and established the State Law and Order Restoration Council (SLORC). More demonstrations and violence followed.

At elections in 1990, Aung San Suu Kyi's National League for Democracy party secured 392 of the 485 seats in parliament but SLORC refused to accept the results. In the years that followed, Aung San Suu Kyi was put under almost permanent house arrest and many of her party and other political activists imprisoned.

In 2002, the government commissioned the construction of a new capital city, called Naypyidaw, or the Abode of Kings, 460 km (300 miles) north of the former capital, Yangon. All government ministries and military officers were relocated there in 2005, a city of imposing buildings and eight-lane highways.

Left: Inscriptions on the base of the Victory Monument in Mahabandula Garden, formerly known as Fytche Square, with the grand old Yangon courthouse in the background.

Opposite top: A poster seller displays images of Aung San Suu Kyi and her father in the streets of Yangon.

Opposite bottom: Colourful key rings are also now on sale.

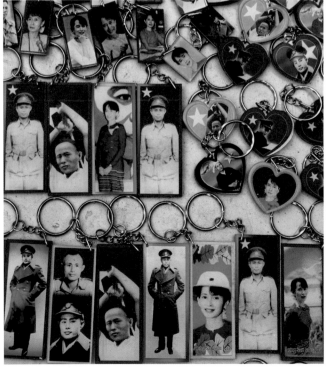

A Time for Optimism

In April 2010, cabinet ministers resigned their military commissions in order to prepare for elections that resulted in Prime Minister Thein Sein being appointed as leader of the Union Solidarity and Development Party. On November 7, 2010, Myanmar held its first elections in 20 years, although Aung San Suu Kyi and her party were not allowed to stand.

In December 2011, US Secretary of State Hillary Clinton made a landmark visit to the country and held meetings with Aung San Suu Kyi and President Thein Sein, resulting in improved relations with the wider world. On 1st April 2012, Aung San Suu Kyi was allowed to take part in parliamentary by-elections. She enjoyed a sweeping victory for her party, The National League for Democracy, and paved the way for further democratic reforms.

The People

M yanmar's population of 56 million is predominantly Bamar but there are also seven other main races, the Chin, Kachin, Kayah, Kayin, Mon, Rakhine and Shan, and 130 recognized minority groups. There is also a significant Chinese presence in the main cities and towns, and several Indian communities. More than 110 languages and dialects are spoken but Myanmar is the state language. Three-quarters of the population reside in small towns and villages where they eke out a living as farmers and merchants.

Opposite: Buddhist nuns crossing a wooden suspension bridge and enjoying a day out at Pwe Kauk Falls, known as Hampshire Falls during the British colonial-era, near Pyin U Lwin.

Below: Shopping in the colourful fresh markets is part of everyday life in Myanmar.

The majority of the Bamar lives in the Ayeyarwaddy basin area and speaks Myanmar, a Shino-Tibetan language. Officially three per cent of Myanmar's population is of Chinese descent but due to a wave of immigration over the past two decades, the true figure is much higher. The original Chinese settlers arrived in the 19th century during British rule; many coming via what was then British Malaya, modern-day Malaysia and Singapore. The Chinese quickly integrated and began to dominate the economy, as they still do today. Myanmar-Chinese have strong communities in Yangon and most urban centres. A new influx of migrants from Yunnan province to Mandalay has resulted in a development boom and it is believed that ethnic Chinese now account for up to 40 % of the city's population.

Indian settlers were also encouraged to come to Myanmar by the British and were employed as civil servants in the administration. However, many were forced out of the country in the early 1960s. Today, those remaining make a living as merchants and moneylenders in Yangon, Mandalay and the colonial-era hill stations of Kalaw and Pyin U Lwin.

For travellers interested in ethnic minorities and their distinctive cultures, Myanmar is endlessly fascinating. To the west, bordering Bangladesh and India is the Chin whose customs once included the facial tattooing of women. Although it has not been practised for many years, a few elderly women with tattoos can still be seen in some villages of the Chin State. Other minorities include the Kayin, also known as the Karen, who for many years have been struggling for an independent state, and the Shan, the country's largest ethnic group. Colourful hill tribes include the Lahu, Lisu, Pa O, Akha and the Kayin Lahwi or Padaung, more commonly referred to as 'long neck' because of the brass rings worn around their necks.

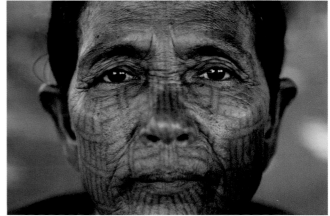

Above: *A few of the older tribal women in Myanmar's western Chin State have striking facial tattoos. The tradition died out years ago.*

Top: *Two young girls selling tissues and sweets to commuters on the ferry across the Yangon River.*

Tanaka – Natural Beauty

One of the most noticeable and enchanting features of Myanmar women is their love of *tanaka*, a natural face powder used as a sunscreen. The perfumed powder comes from the wood apple tree (*Limonia acidissima*) and is for sale in all markets. Prepared by grinding the bark into a paste on a flat stone with a little water, it is applied to the cheeks, often in creative ways, and dries as a pale yellow powder that exerts a mesmerizing glow – circles of pure light illuminating sun-blessed skin. Small children are also routinely covered with tanaka as a sun block. Today, tanaka is also available in paste form but many women still prefer to grind their own.

This page: In Myanmar, tanaka is said to be the secret of a lady's beautiful skin. Different grades of wood are sold in the markets and considerable care is taken to choose the best and most fragrant.

Religion

The majority of the population of Myanmar practises Theravada Buddhism while five per cent are Christian, four per cent Muslim and a small percentage Animist and Hindu.

Below: Myanmar people are deeply religious. Here, worshippers kneel and pray in front of Buddha images at Sule Paya in the heart of Yangon.

Buddhism is thought to have been brought to Myanmar during the third century B.C. through a mission sent from India by King Asoka. Monks from Sri Lanka are also believed to have arrived in the country during the sixth and 10th centuries. Today, Buddhism pervades Myanmar society and there are over 500,000 monks and nuns, and 50,000 monastic communities. Every young man is expected to become a novice monk for a short period of his life between the age of ten and 20. Many orphans and children from poor families are also taken in and cared for by temples.

One of the most intriguing aspects of religion in Myanmar is the worship of 37 nats or spirits. These nats are believed to be the souls of people who died violently and continue to wander the earth. One of the most powerful nats is Mahagiri, who is honoured at a shrine on Mount Popa near Bagan. Dozens of other minor nats that inhabit trees, rivers, mountains and homes are also worshipped.

Animism is practised by several hill tribes but many indigenous groups, such as the Chin, Kayin and Kachin, were targeted by the missionaries during the 19th and 20th centuries and converted to Christianity. Although there is a strong Muslim presence in Yangon, the majority are to the west in Rakhine State, bordering Bangladesh.

Left: Buddhist nuns in their colourful pink robes taking food donated during alms collection back to the temple.

Above: At Tharabar Gate in Bagan's old town locals often stop for a blessing from the brother and sister nat spirits guarding each side of the road.

Myanmar Cuisine

Authentic Myanmar cuisine is an intriguing blend of influences from neighbouring India, China and Thailand. Adventurous diners can also explore a range of regional flavours from the Shan State in the north-east to Rakhine in the west.

Below: *An enticing spread usually comprises several different dishes served at the same time, accompanied by steamed vegetables and rice.*

A typical meal shared between diners will include an array of dishes, such as a meat or fish curry, a sour soup and salad, and a selection of steamed vegetables with a spicy dip or relish, usually all served together and accompanied by the staple grain, rice. The dominant flavours of Myanmar cuisine are fried shallots, garlic, turmeric, ginger and tamarind – used to introduce a sour note to soups – the indispensable *nam pya ye* or fish sauce, *ngapi* (shrimp paste) and, of course, fiery chillies. Pulses, such as butter beans and split peas, are also common ingredients while sesame seeds and peanuts are often liberally used in salads as, for example, *lahpet tohk*, a mix of pickled tea leaves, peanuts, toasted sesame seeds, garlic, tomato, chilli, dried shrimps and ginger.

Despite the liking for large shared meals of complex flavour combinations, if anything can be considered the

Left: Ladies selling 'mohinga' at a shop in central Yangon. The tasty fish soup is one of the country's most popular dishes.

Below: This vendor's bowls of food for sale on the streets in Yangon are a mix of culinary influences from Myanmar and India.

national dish of Myanmar it is *mohinga*, a delicious one bowl wonder of fragrant fish soup ladled over rice noodles and enjoyed for breakfast, lunch or dinner. Desserts include *shwe kyi*, a rich semolina and coconut milk pudding, *kyauk kyaw*, a type of coconut milk jelly, and *thagu byin*, a tapioca pudding sweetened with cane sugar. At Thingyan New Year celebrations, rice flour dumplings known as *mon lone yea paw* are a traditional sweet treat.

Regional Influences

Indian food is popular and widely available in Myanmar but the best is in Yangon where many restaurants offer staples, such as biryani chicken, chapatis and dahl. Samosas and other favourites are also sold as roadside snacks. The Chinese influence is evident in the noodle dishes, a type of porridge made with rice and a flavourful meat stock, and *mantou*, sweet or savoury steamed buns with a variety of fillings. One of many ethnic dishes loved by all is the Shan *khao swè*, rice noodles with minced chicken or pork, onions, garlic, tomatoes and chilli, as well as another Shan classic, *tohu thote*, a tasty salad with chickpea tofu.

Market Values

Daily visits to the market are central to the Myanmar way of life. For the visitor too, it's an essential experience. In the early morning and late afternoon, side streets are transformed into a canvas brushed with strokes of colour reminiscent of Gauguin's palette and every glance or tentative inquiry is greeted with a capacious smile. Squatting among nests of verdant green produce, traders attract customers as eager for gossip as they are for fresh produce and a bargain.

Tea and Betel

Myanmar people are enthusiastic tea drinkers. On almost every street there is a tea shop or a cluster of plastic stools and low tables where locals enjoy sipping tea and indulging in a few pastries while they put the world to rights.

The chewing of betel nut in Myanmar is certainly the most unappealing habit but extremely popular with men and women alike. Sellers stand behind their street-side counters preparing small wraps of the mildly stimulating mixture. Mobile vendors also ply the streets with wooden trays around their necks, each well stocked with the essential ingredients. Stained orange lips and teeth as well as the ubiquitous rust-coloured splats on the pavements are all signs of betel chewing. The nut itself is from the areca palm while the leaf in which it is wrapped comes from the piper betel vine. With well-practised fingers the street vendors place a leaf on a board, dip a piece of wooden dowel into a pot of slaked lime and brush the leaf with it, add slices of nut, dried tobacco leaves, cloves, cumin seeds or cardamom to personal taste and wrap it all together. The deftly folded emerald-green packets of the 'local chew' are sold for just a few kyat.

Above: Ladies in a local market picking the biggest and tastiest deep-fried crickets. The wild food is a popular high protein snack.

Right: Myanmar people are prodigious tea drinkers. Seated at low street-side tables and chairs, they enjoy the local brew served with samosas, cakes and sweet treats throughout the day and night.

Above: Hledan market in a suburb of Yangon is just one of many vibrant street markets where locals shop for fresh vegetables.

Left: The chewing of betel nut is a widespread habit. Vendors can be found selling the 'local chew' every few metres.

Festivals and Events

The many colourful festivals and events held throughout the year in Myanmar are closely linked to Buddhism, the spirit world and the lunar calendar. Highlights include New Year festivities and *nat pwe* or spirit festivals.

Opposite top: *Myanmar celebrates a seemingly endless number of temple and full moon festivals, such as this one at the Shwedagon Paya.*

The Myanmar New Year celebration of Thingyan takes place during April, the hottest and dustiest time of year. Although it is a time to express religious devotion, it is also seen as an opportunity to let off steam and is marked by the enthusiastic throwing of water from dawn till dusk. Water is also used symbolically to wash away bad luck. During this time people carry pots of water to the temple in order to bathe the images of Buddha; homes are cleaned and younger family members wash the hair of their elders as a mark of respect.

According to local beliefs, the King of Celestial Beings, Thagya–min, pays a visit to homes at this time of year. He carries with him two books, one covered with dog-skin in which he records the names of those who have committed sins and the other bound with gold, for those who have carried out good deeds. The spirit is welcomed by all people and a small, wide-mouthed, earthenware pot containing Eugenia leaves and flowers is left as an offering.

The largest *nat pwe* is held in August at Taung Pyone village, just north of Mandalay. For several days preceding and following the night of the full moon, the event honours two of the most popular nat spirits, the brothers Shwe Phyin Gyi and Shwe Phyin Lay who are said to have been executed by King Anawrahta in the 11th century for not assisting with the construction of a zedi. Tens of thousands of people visit the festival which includes a circus, music, dance and fortune tellers. On the fourth day, locals partake in the ritual bathing of the images of the two nat princes and a procession to Shwe Ta Chaung stream, known as the golden stream.

Above: *On special religious days, the temples draw devout Buddhists in their thousands who come to pray and meditate.*

Opposite below: *As part of their religious observance, Buddhists light candles and incense, adorn Buddha images with flowers and cleanse them with a ritual bathing.*

Arts and Crafts

Years of isolation, lack of development and a strong sense of cultural identity have been favourable to Myanmar's arts and crafts. Lifestyles and traditions which are fast disappearing elsewhere in the region are still alive and well in Myanmar. Many crafts, such as stone carving, bronze casting and the making of parasols, are inextricably linked to Buddhism. Others, including handmade, simple earthenware pottery, silk and cotton textiles, and lacquerware are part of everyday life.

Opposite: *Lacquerware is one of Myanmar's most celebrated and highly skilled arts. The intricately engraved works are also one of the most popular purchases for visitors.*

Below: *Making traditional earthenware water jars is more widespread here than in other South-East Asian countries. Here a woman at pottery sheds near Bago makes her wares.*

Pottery

Myanmar has a long tradition of pottery making which continues since cooking pots, water jars and water storage vessels are still in high demand. Pot making areas include O Bo village near Mandalay in the Sagaing district and the neighbouring villages of Nwe Nyein, Shwe Khun, Shwe Tiek and Malar in the Shwebo district. The four thriving villages are more commonly known as Kyauk Myuang (actually a nearby town) and have produced huge, glazed, water storage jars for centuries. Nearer to Yangon, for many years Twante and Bago have been – and still are – important centres of pottery production.

Lacquerware

Lacquerware is Myanmar's most famous craft and has been produced in and around Bagan for centuries. Traditional items include highly ornate betel boxes and ceremonial wares. Vessels made from wood or bamboo are coated with multiple layers of lacquer, a resin obtained by tapping a tree (*Gluta usitata*) for milky sap which turns black when exposed to air. Dyes of various colours are often mixed into the resin so complex designs can be engraved through the

layers. Decoration includes intricate patterns and scenes from the Buddhist scriptures. The product of many skilled hands, a single piece of work can take weeks, even months to complete.

Stone Carving

In Mandalay, the area in the vicinity of 45th and 84th streets close to the Mahamuni Paya, is lined with stone-carving workshops. Here, skilled craftsmen attack pure white marble with angle grinders and drills to create enigmatic Buddha images. Carvings of all sizes, from the smallest keepsake to monumental three-metre (ten-foot) high statues, can be seen at all stages of production.

Bronze Casting

Using a process that dates back thousands of years called lost-wax casting, craftsmen in Myanmar create beautiful bronze Buddhas. First a detailed wax image is made and encased in earthenware clay. The mould is then heated to burn out the wax and the bronze poured in. Foundries in Mandalay are renowned for producing high quality bronzes that are commissioned for temples all over the country.

Above: Before a Buddha can be cast in bronze, the artist first makes a detailed image in wax.

Top right: Stone carvers in Mandalay hack away at marble with power tools but manage to produce works of exquisite beauty.

Woven Textiles

Cotton and silk *longyis* or sarongs are produced on hand-operated and mechanical looms in the main production centre of Amarapura and Mandalay but there are also many factories in the Inle area, Rakhine State and Mon State. Myanmar men favour a simple check pattern, while women prefer bright colours and ornate patterns including the traditional Bamar Acheik design, a horizontal band of waves and hooks.

Below: At In Phaw Khon on Inle Lake weavers use threads made from water lotus to produce a unique fabric that ends up as garments in high-end boutiques in the west.

Right: A Padaung long-neck woman wearing her distinctive brass neck rings sits weaving textiles in a workshop at Inle Lake.

Left: The once dying art of marionette theatre was saved by tourism. The puppets can be bought as souvenirs in Mandalay and Yangon.

Below: The Mandalay Marionette Theatre is an intimate space where visitors can enjoy an entertaining nightly show performed by a troop of talented puppeteers.

Marionettes

Once a popular performing art in the royal courts of the 1800s, marionette theatre fell from favour and almost vanished in Myanmar. The popular Mandalay Marionette Theatre, which gives nightly performances, is widely credited with doing much to save the traditions but it is still seen as a dying art. Manipulated by a troop of puppeteers, performances include several characters in tales of the Buddha's life and historic legends. Traditional handmade puppets, old and new, are widely available in tourist areas across the country.

Whackin' White Cheroots

From the smoky smiles of young ladies and puffing trishaw drivers to pensive pipe-smoking grannies, tobacco is still as popular now as when Kipling immortalized a Burmese girl named Supi-yaw-lat "a-smokin' of a whackin' white cheroot" in 'The Road to Mandalay'. Although huge white cheroots are still common, the smoke of choice is often slender and green. Made in workshops around Bago and in the Shan State, each cheroot is hand-rolled in a matter of seconds.

Chapter 2: Yangon and its Environs

The former capital of Yangon is located in Lower Myanmar at the convergence of the Bago and Yangon rivers and 30 km (18 miles) from the Gulf of Mottama. Once heralded as the jewel in South-East Asia's crown, today Yangon is an uncut diamond patiently waiting for the hand of a skilled craftsman to bring back its sparkle. But it is the city's neglected colonial-era architecture, temples and trishaws, and bustling markets that create its unique character and make it so appealing.

Above: The Karaweik on the eastern shore of Kandawgyi Lake is, a reproduction of a royal barge in the shape of a legendary bird.

Left: In the early morning and late afternoon, impromptu markets set up along the streets of central Yangon.

Opposite page: In the 19th century Captain Alexander Fraser of the Bengal Engineers created the Victorian style layout of the city streets and declared the Sule Paya the centre of Yangon.

Shwedagon Paya

It is impossible not to be moved by the beauty of the Shwedagon Paya. Located on Singuttara Hill and rising 100 m (328 ft) from its base to pierce the sky, the golden zedi dominates Yangon and can be seen from over 80 km (50 miles) away.

The term paya means 'holy one' or 'holy place' in Myanmar language. Within the expansive temple grounds, the ambience changes throughout the day and it is well worth visiting the paya on more than one occasion. Open from 4 a.m. until around 10 p.m., the temple can be accessed by a stairway at one of four entrances, each lined with shops selling religious imagery and souvenirs. For those who cannot manage the climb there is also a lift at one of the entrances.

This page: The west gate of the Shwedagon Paya is guarded by two huge mythical lion-like creatures known as 'chinthe', as are the other three gates. Upon entering, visitors are faced with a long stairway leading up to the temple.

This page: Two visits to the Shwedagon Paya are essential. At the crack of dawn, visitors will see many Buddhist monks and nuns in moments of reflection, prayer and meditation; by night, when the sky darkens and the spotlights come on, the magnificent zedi can be experienced in all its glittering golden glory.

This page: In the heart of central Yangon, the Sule Paya is one of the city's most recognizable landmarks. The central 46-m (151-ft) octagonal zedi and the small shops that encircle it act as a traffic roundabout in the centre of a busy intersection.

Left: A trio of Buddha images at Sule Paya have been adorned with silken robes by worshippers during one of Myanmar's many religious festivals.

Below: Located in a Yangon suburb, the 70-m (230-ft) reclining Buddha at Chauk Htat Gyi Temple is an impressive sight. Built in 1966, the soles of the feet are embellished with 108 auspicious Buddhist symbols.

Yangon Markets

For atmosphere and photographic opportunities, visit the expansive Hledan Market at the intersection of Insein and University roads, or Theingyi Zei on Shwedagon Paya Road. Both markets offer an insight into life in Yangon and also sell just about everything imaginable. It's also worth exploring side streets around Theingyi Zei in the late afternoon, as there are many fresh produce vendors in the area. Thiri Mingalar Zei on the outskirts of the city is another excellent morning market. Tourist trinkets and textiles can be found at Bogyoke Market, also known as Scott Market.

These pages: A stroll through a Yangon market is an experience to savour. The bounty of fresh ingredients are laid out like paints on an artist's palette, and the air filled with the sound of friendly banter and the persistent sales pitch of vendors.

Colonial-era Architecture

Yangon has some of the finest examples of British colonial-era buildings in Asia. Most have fallen into a state of disrepair, nevertheless they do add to the city's special charm and hopefully will soon benefit from restoration.

Top right: Yangon's colonial-era ambience is very much alive at its most celebrated hotel, The Strand. This grand old dame dates from 1901 and has welcomed distinguished guests including Somerset Maugham, George Orwell, Sir Noel Coward and Rudyard Kipling, to name but a few. After a period of decline, the stately hotel was saved and has now been restored to its former glory with cool marble bathrooms, teakwood floors, lazy ceiling fans and traditional Burmese lacquerware. Today's travellers still enjoy the pleasures for which it was once renowned: a welcoming and knowledgeable General Manager, personalized service, tempting afternoon teas and the distinct feeling that you are part of its rich history.

Below right: A fine example of colonial-era architecture at the corner of Strand Road. It awaits careful restoration to bring back its splendour like the stately Strand Hotel.

Circular Train

A recommended trip during a stay in Yangon is a ride on the circular train, a reliable German engine plus battered coaches, that regularly leaves the city's Central Station on a 50 km (31 mile) loop through the suburbs. The dimly lit carriages of the local commuter service act as a stage for an intimate performance of daily life in Yangon. With the cast regularly changing at each of the 39 stations en route and with backdrops that include scenes from the inner city, vibrant markets and verdant rice fields, the three-hour journey is time well spent. Trains leave every 45 minutes and tickets are available from platform 7 at the Central Station. Foreign passengers are required to show their passports.

Below: The circular train waits to leave Yangon Central Station. The small fare charged for the ticket is worth every penny but passengers will end up crammed in with friendly market traders and their huge baskets of vegetables. It's all part of the experience on this wonderful journey around the city.

Around Yangon

Although Yangon has much for travellers to discover, it also makes an excellent base from which to visit nearby sights and attractions. Highlights within easy reach of the city include the deeply moving British War Cemetery, the town of Bago and Myanmar's most sacred religious site, the Golden Rock.

This page: Formerly known as Pegu by the British, the town of Bago is 80 km (50 miles) from Yangon and a convenient rest stop on the way to the Golden Rock. Attractions for visitors include Shwemawdaw Paya (right), the Four Figure Paya, a 76 m (250 ft) reclining Buddha at Naung Daw Gyi Mya Tha Lyaung (below), the Snake Monastery, home to an enormous python, and cheroot factories.

This page: The magnificent Golden Rock, also known as Mount Kyaikhtiyo, is one of Myanmar's most sacred Buddhist sites. Roughly three hours' drive east of Yangon, it is a place of pilgrimage for Buddhists from all over Asia who come to pray and rub gold leaf on the precariously perched rock. As with many sites of pilgrimage, getting there requires effort. A nail-biting truck ride takes you halfway up the mountain, then the rest of the steep climb is done on foot. If you want to experience both sunset and sunrise here, make sure you stay at the hotels at the top – just a 10-minute walk from the actual site.

Chapter 3: Central Myanmar

Myanmar's heartland is home to its biggest attraction – Bagan. Here, travellers can explore the many ancient ruins by horse and cart or view the expansive site from above in a hot air balloon. Cruise ships also arrive at Bagan having sailed down river from Mandalay.

Bagan

Lying 140 km (90 miles) south-west of Mandalay on the banks of the Ayeyarwaddy, ancient Bagan is one of the highlights of a visit to Myanmar. Bagan was the capital of the first empire and, at its peak from A.D. 1057 to the mid-1200s, was home to over 4,000 Buddhist temples. Although many ruins collapsed during a powerful earthquake in 1975, 2,217 important sites remain. The main temple sites and ruins are scattered across a 40-km^2 (16-sq. mile) plain.

This page: Built around 1105 for King Kyanzittha, the Ananda Paya is one of the masterpieces of Bagan. Within the temple four 9.5 m (31 ft) images represent the Buddha after he attained nirvana. The north and south facing images have the 'dhammachakka mudra' hand position symbolizing Buddha's first sermon.

This page: Dhammayangyi Temple, the largest structure in Bagan, was built for the ruthless King Narathu who reigned from 1167-70 and is said to have murdered his own father so that he could ascend the throne. The temple passages feature golden Buddha images and walls adorned with the remains of beautiful frescoes.

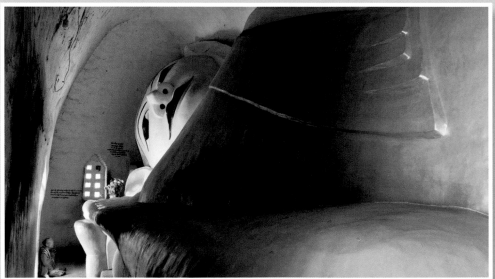

Above and above right: The intricate zedi at Mahabodi temple houses a large golden Buddha and is modelled after its namesake in Bodhgaya, India.

Left: A woman prays in front of a reclining Buddha at Manuha Paya.

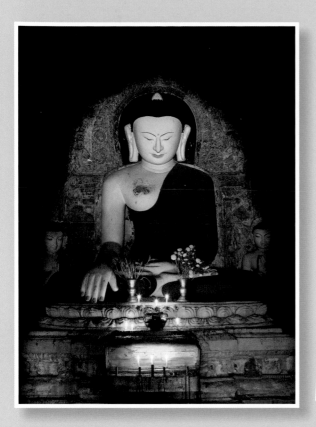

Left: A Buddha illuminated by candlelight at Nagayon Hpaya.

Below: Shwegugyi temple, built for King Alaungsithu in AD. 1140 has many enigmatic Buddhas and detailed frescoes.

Right: A horse and carriage passing through Tharabar Gate in the old town. Many visitors to Bagan choose this leisurely form of transport to explore the monuments.

Below and below right: Frescoes on the stuccoed interior of the Sulimani Guphaya, one of the top attractions among the hundreds of temples and pagodas at Bagan. The temple's apt name means 'crowning jewel'.

Right: Towering above the other monuments of Bagan, the magnificent white Thatbyinnyu temple was built for King Alaungsithu (1113-1163). From the terraces visitors enjoy a panoramic view of Bagan and the distant hills.

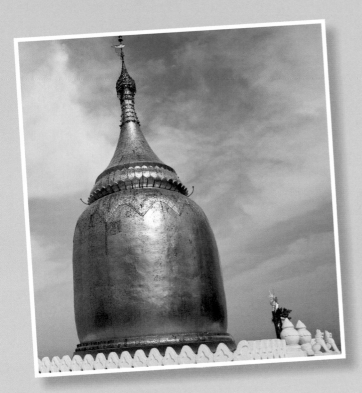

Above: Bupaya, an unusual golden gourd-shaped zedi on the eastern bank of the Ayeyarwaddy was built in 1975 to replace the original after it fell in the river following a powerful earthquake.

Right: Several temples at Bagan can be climbed to gain a view of the surrounding area. At sunrise and sunset, Shwesandaw Paya and Pyathada Paya draw the crowds.

This page: One of the best and most inspiring ways to see Bagan is from the air. 'Balloons Over Bagan' offer hour-long sunrise and sunset flights in hot air balloons that float over the thousand-year-old ruins and temple spires. The once-in-a-lifetime experience is the perfect way to appreciate the sheer scale and majesty of one of the world's most important religious sites. Following a magical flight, the landing is softened by a celebratory glass of Champagne.

This page: For many visitors to Myanmar, cruising down the Ayeyarwaddy provides the perfect combination of luxury and adventure. The 'Road to Mandalay' run by Orient Express Hotels is a palatial cruise ship that plies the mighty river from as far north as Bhamo, down to Mandalay and on to Bagan. Passengers pass through some of the country's most beautiful scenery, stopping en route to explore towns and important cultural sites, such as Sagaing, Pyin U Lwin hill station and the temples of Bagan. Evenings are spent on board enjoying vivid sunsets from the deck, fine dining, insightful lectures on local culture and a variety of entertainments.

Chapter 4: Eastern Myanmar

In the east, the many historic wonders and beautiful temples of Mandalay and the surrounding area make it an essential part of any travel itinerary. At Inle Lake it is hotels on stilts above the water, boat trips through floating gardens and bustling hill tribe markets that are the main sights to be seen.

Inle Lake

Inle Lake is one of Myanmar's most popular tourist attractions. Located 35 km (21 miles) from the town of Heho in the Shan State, the shallow lake covers over 110 km^2 (40 sq. miles) and is surrounded by villages inhabited by Intha, Shan and other ethnic groups and hill tribes including Pa O and Padaung. Most visitors stay on stilted resorts over the water and around the edge of the lake, and make excursions by boat to colourful morning markets in nearby villages.

Above: At Inle Lake, life is waterborne. In this unique destination there are waterside temples, floating markets, floating gardens growing vegetables, and stilted villages and hotels above the water.

Left: In the early morning, young monks paddle boats from house to house collecting alms from devout Buddhists.

Above: *A trio of fishermen using distinctive traditional fishing baskets. The large conical baskets are pushed to the bottom of the shallow lake and the fish caught within are speared.*

Left: *Phaung Daw U Paya is the most sacred temple in the Shan State. In September or October, the Buddha images are paraded around the lake in a boat.*

Mandalay

Situated on the banks of the Ayeyarwaddy, Mandalay is Myanmar's second largest city. In recent years it has boomed, attracting thousands of Chinese immigrants, a frenzy of construction and a rapid increase in traffic. As a result it has lost much of its former charm but among the chaos are many attractions and it makes an excellent base from which to explore Sagaing, U Bein's teak bridge and the former hill station of Pyin U Lwin.

Above: In recent years, Mandalay has boomed and the once traffic-free streets now buzz with motorcycles and cars.

Right: Two huge white 'chinthe', a mythical lion-like creature, stand guard at the southwest entrance to Mandalay Hill.

Opposite page: Rows of white zedis at Kuthodaw Paya. From the top of Mandalay Hill, visitors can take in a panoramic view of the city.

Above: *A fisherman rows across Taungthaman Lake near U Bein's Bridge towards the Spiral Temple.*

Right and opposite page: *15 km (9 miles) from Mandalay at Amarapura is the 12- km (3/4 mile) U Bein's Bridge, the world's longest teak bridge. The bridge connects two small communities and spans a vast area which during the dry season is used for farming peanuts, sesame and other cash-crops. When the rains come, it floods and provides a daily catch for local fisherman. Farmers can also be seen rounding up their ducks in the late evening. In years of excessive rain it is not unknown for the bridge to be completely submerged. The middle section includes concrete posts, replacements for teak pillars that were washed away a few years ago.*

This page: *Shwenandaw Kyaung is an exquisitely carved teak temple and one of Mandalay's most important historic temples. Built in the 19th century for King Mindon, it is the only surviving section of the former royal palace complex.*

This page: Mandalay was the last seat of Myanmar royalty and home to the royal palace. Unfortunately, the original buildings were destroyed by fire in World War II as British forces moved against the occupying Japanese army. The buildings that stand on the site today are a reconstruction.

This page: *A short distance from Mandalay, Sagaing Hill is scattered with temples and golden zedis. At Umin Thounzeh temple, 45 Buddha statues sit within a crescent-shaped chamber. The nearby town of Sagaing is situated on the western bank of the Ayeyarwaddy River and in AD1315 was the capital of an independent Shan Kingdom.*

This page: An hour's boat ride boat down the Ayeyarwaddy from Mandalay is the town of Mingun and the monumental Mantara Gyi Paya, destroyed by a massive earthquake in 1838. At the river's edge, steps lead to Settawya Paya, a vaulted shrine housing the footprint of Buddha.

Above: In Pyin U Lwin, the clock tower gifted by Queen Victoria and horse and carriages are a reminder of the former British colonial-era hill station's history.

Left: Buddhist nuns enjoying a day out and taking photographs at Pwe Kauk Falls, once known as Hampshire Falls, near Pyin U Lwin.

Opposite: The formal National Kandawgyi Gardens were established in 1915 by the English botanist, Alex Rodgers. Covering 176 hectares (435 acres), the beautiful gardens are home to almost 500 plants species.

Above: Mahanthtoo Kanthat Pagoda is another of the many attractions in the Pyin U Lwin area.

Right: The Chinese Buddha image at the temple of Chan Tak, located a few kilometres from Pyin U Lwin.

Chapter 5: North-western Myanmar

A truly fascinating part of the country, the northwest region offers attractions for cultural travellers and beach lovers alike. Highlights include an adventurous river trip from Sittwe to the Mrauk U to explore historic temples and lazy days on Ngapali Beach for the perfect end to a memorable trip.

Ngapali Beach

Fringed by gently swaying coconut palms, Ngapali Beach is an idyllic three-kilometre (two-mile) stretch of white sand lapped by the clear waters of the Bay of Bengal. Just 45 minutes flying time from Yangon, the area is quickly attracting developers keen to exploit its natural beauty. Visitors can enjoy lazy days on the beach, snorkelling trips, watching fishermen land their catch at daybreak, and sampling delicious seafood in the restaurants that line the beach road.

Right: For years, Ngapali Beach has been South-East Asia's best kept secret; an idyllic stretch of white sand enjoyed by Yangon's middle class and a handful of expats. Even now it still retains the charm and tranquillity that neighbouring Thailand's beach resorts lost 20 years ago. Boat trips can also be taken further up the coast where the beaches are totally deserted.

These pages: One of Ngapali's attractions is that it is still a working beach. Fishing boats anchor off the shoreline throughout the day, heading out to sea at around 5 p.m. and returning at daybreak. The catch is mostly tiny fish which are laid out on bright blue netting to dry in the sun. A few mackerel, barracuda, and squid are also landed.

Sittwe

Sitting at the mouth of the Kaladan River, Sittwe is an important port in Rakhine State. Its close proximity to Bangladesh and a bustling fish market give the town a unique ambience. The British forces landed at Sittwe in 1825 and the small fishing village quickly became an important trading centre. Today, it is the starting point for boat trips to Mrauk U.

This page: In the early mornings and late afternoons, Sittwe's market comes alive with trishaw drivers angling for business, and fisherman trying to sell their meagre catch.

Opposite page: A pleasant evening can be spent on the jetty of this busy little fishing town watching the boats come and go.

Mrauk U

The former capital of Rakhine State in western Myanmar, Mrauk U – pronounced Mror Oo – is an atmospheric town reached by a six-hour boat journey from Sittwe. The town and surrounding countryside are scattered with temple ruins, many of which are still used by local people and monks. Travel another couple of hours up the Lemro River and you'll enter the lower reaches of the Chin State. Most of this mountainous area is currently off limits to travellers but a handful of ethnic villages can now be visited with a guide. The main attractions for tourists, in addition to the outstanding natural beauty, are the few remaining Chin women who sport impressive facial tattoos.

Above: *Buddhas in a passageway of Kothaung Paya, the 'shrine of 90,000 images'. The temple which dates from 1553 is the largest in Mrauk U.*

Top: *The tradition of facial tattooing among the tribes of the Chin State was carried out on girls between the ages of seven and 15, a painful process to endure that is no longer practised.*

This page: The approach to Mrauk U is made by boat. Two ancient zedis atop a hill are the first sign that this is no ordinary town. Many days can be spent here exploring hundreds of ruins in the area. One of the most impressive sites is Kothaung Paya, seen here across the rice fields. In addition to the images that line the passageways, the outer terrace has 108 small zedis.

Right: In the 16th and 17th centuries Mrauk U was a wealthy city within Arakan, a powerful independent state encompassing the fertile valleys of Kaladan and Lemro. Its proximity to the Bay of Bengal and India made it an important trading centre. However, in 1784, Arakan was attacked by King Bodawpaya and became part of Myanmar's Rakhine State. Mrauk U is also renowned as the site of the first Anglo-Burmese War in 1825 but after victory, the British moved their troops to Sittwe. Today, Mrauk U's former glories can be seen from a hill near Ratanabon Paya, the most popular spot to enjoy the sunset. Ringed by smaller zedis, Ratanabon's bulk dominates the view. The temple was built in 1612 by Min Khamoung and became known as the 'pile of jewels' because it was rumoured to have a hoard of gold hidden within.

Getting About

Getting around can be challenging. Although a few main highways have been upgraded, roads in rural Myanmar can be rough. Most visitors choose to use the domestic airlines to hop from one destination to another.

The country's main gateway is Yangon International Airport. Located in Mingaladon Township, 15 km (10 miles) north of central Yangon, it features an international terminal that was completed in 2007. The original building now serves as the domestic terminal. On arrival, travellers can hire an unmetered taxi or minivan to the centre of Yangon, paying the driver at the destination.

There are several domestic airports in Myanmar served by a number of local airlines including Air Bagan, Air Mandalay and Asian Wings Airways. Routes include Yangon to Nyuang U (for Bagan), Thandwe (for Ngapali Beach), Sittwe, Heho (for Inle Lake), Keng Tung, Myitkyina and Putao. Flights often make brief stops at another airport en route. During the peak season of November to February, advance booking is essential for both international and domestic flights as they often run at full capacity.

Visitors to Myanmar can also enter by land borders with Thailand at Mae Sai-Tachilek crossing and the Mae Sot-Myawaddy crossing. However, these border points can often close temporarily and with little notice so checking in advance is important. Travellers entering overland must also exit by the same point.

In Myanmar only pristine dollar notes are accepted. This applies throughout the country. Even the slightest tear, crease or pen mark and the bill will be refused. You are advised to get plenty of brand new bills to exchange for local *kyat* at banks.

Traffic in Yangon is light considering the population is around 4.5 million. This is due to restrictions on the

importation of vehicles. There are no motorcycles at all as they are said to cause too many accidents and were outlawed in the city several years ago, so the majority of people in Yangon travel by bus, unmetered taxi, trishaw or bicycle, or they simply walk. Of course, all this makes it a very pleasant city to get around. Taxis are cheap, trishaws fun and walking around Yangon with a camera, a pure joy.

Bus travel in Myanmar is cheap but uncomfortable unless you are travelling on one of the few main highways as many roads are potholed or severely degraded. Buses can also be in bad condition, cramped and with a driver whose road skills may leave much to be desired. A good alternative is to hire a private guide and minivan.

Myanmar has an extensive railway network with 4,300 km (2,700 miles) of track on which run trains with first class facilities and sleeping berths for night journeys. However, the railways have suffered from many years of little or no investment so travellers using the system must be prepared to move at a sedate pace. Typically, a trip from Yangon to Mandalay should take around 14 hours. Delays are a guaranteed part of the experience but the rewards can be great as routes often travel through spectacular scenery, particularly the line from Mandalay north to Myitkina.

Luxury cruises down the Ayeyarwaddy are extremely popular and there are now several companies offering tours ranging from three days to two weeks. The cruises typically include all domestic flights and transfers, meals and sightseeing itineraries which may include highlights in Bagan, Mandalay and Mingun.

Left: Up country, it can often feel like stepping back in time. In Bagan, Inwa, Pyin U Lwin and Mrauk U, visitors can explore the sights at a leisurely pace in a rickety horse and carriage. Locals also use them for everyday transport and bullock carts are common.

Opposite: Across Myanmar, the trishaw is still a cheap and popular means of transport. Traffic in the former capital has gradually increased but is expected to grow rapidly as the economy starts to take off. The traffic jam, once unheard of, is already a reality of city life.

Contact details

The following websites proved useful information for organizing your trip to Myanmar.

There are many tour operators offering services in Myanmar including: Exotissimo: www.exotissimo.com; Diethelm Travel: www.diethelmtravel.com; Asia Holidays, a member of Phoenix Voyages: www.phoenixvoyages.com; Road to Mandalay cruises: www.orient-express.com

For a bespoke travel experience, the award-winning and independent Good News Travels can organize travel and tours in Yangon and beyond: FMI Centre, 4th Floor, Unit 18, Building No. 380, Bogyoke Aung San Rd, Yangon (near The Traders Hotel and Scott Market). Visit the website www.myanmargoodnewstravel.com. Email: goodnewstravels@gmail.com.

If you require a driver and guide in Yangon or for trips further afield, Mr Thant Zin is highly recommended by the author. Tel: 09 5097463 or 959 5097463. Email: thantzin.k31@gmail.com

Websites of interest
The Commonwealth War Graves Commission: www.cwgc.org; Balloons Over Bagan: www.easternsafaris.com; The Strand Hotel: www.ghmhotels.com

Airlines
Air Bagan: www.airbagan.com; Air Mandalay: www.airmandalay.com; Thai Airways: www.thaiairways.com; Bangkok Airways: www.bangkokair.com; AirAsia: www.airasia.com

Bibliography and Recommended Reading
George Orwell, re-issued 2009, *Burmese Days*, Penguin Classics; Emma Larkin, 2011, *Finding George Orwell in Burma*, Granta Books; Amitav Ghosh, New edition 2002, *The Glass Palace*, Flamingo; Michael Aung-Thwin, 2012, *A History of Myanmar Since Ancient Times: Traditions and Transformations*, Reaktion Books; Pamela Gutman, 2001, *Burma's Lost Kingdoms: Splendours of Arakan*, Orchid Press; Tin Cho Chaw, 2008, *Hsa Ba Burmese Cookbook*, Grassblades Ltd; Mick Shippen, 2005, *Traditional Ceramics of South-East Asia*, A&C Black.

Acknowledgements
Many thanks to Mr Didier Belmonte, General Manager of The Strand, Craig Powell and Yinn Mar Nyo at the Traders Hotel, Yangon, William Myatwunna at Good News Travels, Brett Melzer at Balloons Over Bagan and Shanthi Regupathy at Grebstad Hicks Communications, Singapore, www.ghcasia.com.

About the Author
Mick Shippen is a freelance writer and photographer who has been based in South-East Asia for 15 years. He travels extensively throughout Asia conducting research for articles and taking photographs for local and international newspapers and magazines. He is the author of three other titles in this series: *Enchanting Cambodia, Enchanting Laos* and *Enchanting Thailand*, as well as of *The Traditional Ceramics of South East Asia*.

He has provided content and images for several leading guidebooks and his work has also appeared in numerous magazines, the *Bangkok Post*, and the *Australian Sunday Telegraph*. Mick's photography is represented by the premium image library Gallery Stock www.gallerystock.com and by the travel stock agency, 4Corners Images www.4cornersimages.com. His images can also be viewed at www.mickshippen.com

Index

Published and distributed in Thailand by Asia Books Co., Ltd
No. 65/66, 65/70, 7th Floor, Chamnan Phenjati Business Center, Rama 9 Road, Huaykwang, Bangkok 10320, Thailand
Tel. (66) 2-715-9000; Fax: (66) 2-715-9197; E-mail: information@asiabooks.com; www.asiabooks.com

First published in the United Kingdom in 2012 by John Beaufoy Publishing,
11 Blenheim Court, 316 Woodstock Road, Oxford OX2 7NS, England
www.johnbeaufoy.com

10 9 8 7 6 5 4 3 2 1

Great care has been taken to maintain the accuracy of the information contained in this work.
However, neither the publishers nor the author can be held responsible for any consequences
arising from the use of the information contained therein.

ISBN 978-1-906780-78-4

Designed by Glyn Bridgewater
Cartography by William Smuts
Project management by Rosemary Wilkinson

Printed and bound in Singapore by Tien Wah Press (Pte) Ltd.

Cover captions:
Back cover (left to right): *Rice harvesting near Sittwe; The stilted houses on Inle Lake; A Padaung long-neck woman
at her loom in a workshop near Inle Lake; The white sands of Ngapali Beach.*
Front cover top (left to right): *A smiling Myanmar woman wearing* tanaka *powder as a sunscreen; Shwedagon Paya
near Yangon; Young Buddhist monks at prayer; A garlanded Buddha image.*
Front cover (centre): *U Bein's Bridge.*
Front cover (bottom): *Zedis at Bagan captured at dusk.*